How to Use t... ...k

This workbook has been written and developed to be used alongside the Lonsdale revision guide, **AQA GCSE Additional Science Essentials**, to help you get the most out of your revision. You can use it if you are studying at Foundation or Higher Tier.

It contains 'quick fire' questions, including multiple-choice questions, matching pair exercises and short answer questions, to test your understanding of the topics covered in the revision guide.

Start by reading through a topic in the revision guide. Make notes, jotting down anything that you think will help you to remember the information. When you have finished, take a short break and then read through your notes. You might even want to try covering them up and writing them out again from memory.

Finally, work through the relevant questions in this workbook without looking at the guide or your notes.

The page headers and sub-headings in this workbook correspond with those in your revision guide, so that you can easily identify the questions that relate to each topic.

Completing the questions will help to reinforce your understanding of the topics covered in the guide and highlight any areas that need further revision.

The answers to the questions in this workbook are available in a separate booklet. There is a box at the end of each page for you to record your score. Don't worry if you get some questions wrong the first time. Just re-read the information in your revision guide and try again.

The tick boxes on the contents page let you track your revision progress: simply put a tick in the box next to each topic when you are confident that you understand it.

Good luck with your exams!

ISBN 978-1-9(

Published by Lonsdale, a division of Huveaux Plc.

© Lonsdale 2007. All rights reserved.
No part of this publication may be reproduced, stored in a retrieval system or transmitted by any means, electronic, mechanical, photocopying, recording or otherwise, without the prior written permission of Lonsdale.

Project Editor: David Mantovani
Cover Design: Angela English
Concept Design: Sarah Duxbury and Helen Jacobs
Design: Lonsdale
Dragon Digital
Little Red Dog Design
Artwork: Lonsdale and HL Studios

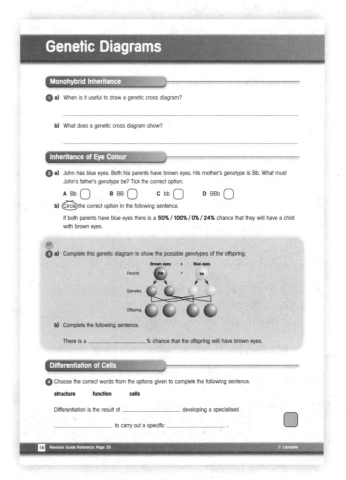

Contents

Contents

The numbers in brackets correspond to the reference numbers on the AQA GCSE Additional Science specification

Biology (handwritten)

Cells

Cells

1 **a)** Circle the correct options in the following sentences.

    i) **Muscles / organs / cells / tissues** are the building blocks of life.

    ii) All **living / material / non-living / plastic** things are made up of cells.

    iii) A living thing is called a(n) **organelle / organism / human / mitochondria**.

  b) Fill in the missing words to complete the following sentence.

    The chemical reactions in a cell are controlled by .... These are found in

    .... and ....

Animal Cells

2 Look at the diagram of an animal cell.

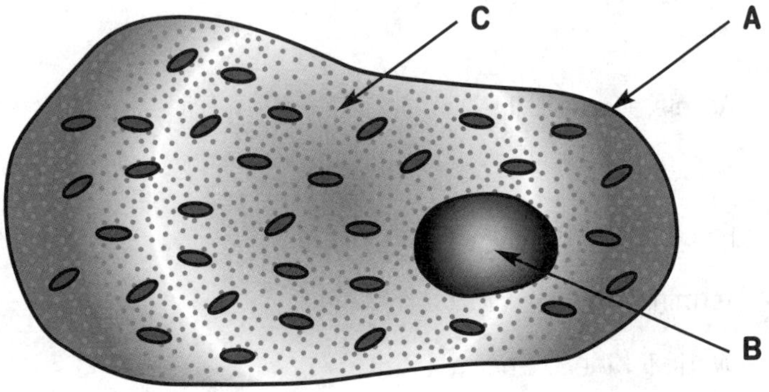

  a) What is the name of part A?
Tick the correct option.

    A Nucleus ☐

    B Cell wall ☑

    C Cell membrane ☐

    D Cytoplasm ☐

  b) What is the name of part B? Tick the correct option.

    A Nucleus ☐   **B** Cell wall ☐

    C Cell membrane ☐   **D** Cytoplasm ☐

  c) What is the name of part C? Tick the correct option.

    A Nucleus ☒   **B** Cell wall ☐

    C Cell membrane ☐   **D** Cytoplasm ☑

Plant Cells

3 Name three differences between an animal cell and a plant cell.

  a) ....

  b) ....

  c) ....

Diffusion & Osmosis

The Movement of Substances

1 Cells have to replace substances that are used up, and remove waste products. They do this by osmosis and diffusion. Choose the correct word(s) from the options given to complete the following sentence.

glucose   **carbon dioxide**   **carbon monoxide**   **oxygen**

One of the waste products that will diffuse out of a cell is ....

Diffusion

2 a) Where does diffusion take place? Tick the correct option.

    A In solids and liquids   ◯

    B In gases only   ◯

    C In solutions and solids   ◯

    D In gases and solutions   ◯

b) When does diffusion take place? Tick the correct option.

    A When there is no concentration gradient   ◯

    B When there is a net movement of particles   ◯

    C When there is movement from a low to a high concentration   ◯

    D When there is melting of a solid   ◯

Osmosis

3 What is 'osmosis'?

....

....

4 What does 'partially permeable' mean? Tick the correct option.

    A Allows all substances to pass through   ◯

    B Allows no substances to pass through   ◯

    C Allows substances to pass through in one direction only   ◯

    D Allows some substances to pass through   ◯

Photosynthesis

Plant Mineral Requirements

1 Fill in the missing words to complete the following sentence.

Plants need mineral _____ , which they absorb from the _____

through their _____ .

2 Why does a plant need nitrates? Tick the correct option.

    A To make DNA and cell membranes   ◯

    B To make enzymes   ◯

    C To form proteins   ◯

    D To make chlorophyll   ◯

3 Choose the correct words from the options given to complete the following sentence.

make DNA and cell membranes   **make enzymes**

form proteins and DNA   **make cholorophyll**

A plant needs magnesium to _____ .

Photosynthesis

4 Which of the following is the correct equation for photosynthesis? Tick the correct option.

    A Glucose + Carbon dioxide ⟶ Oxygen + Water   ◯

    B Glucose + Oxygen ⟶ Carbon monoxide + Water   ◯

    C Glucose + Water ⟶ Carbon dioxide + Oxygen   ◯

    D Carbon dioxide + Water ⟶ Glucose + Oxygen   ◯

5 a) Apart from carbon dioxide and water, what two other factors are required for photosynthesis?

    i) _____

    ii) _____

b) i) What is the name of the pigment that absorbs the Sun's energy during photosynthesis?

_____

    ii) Where is this pigment found?

_____

Factors Affecting Photosynthesis

Factors Affecting Photosynthesis

1. Which of the following are factors that can limit the rate of photosynthesis? Tick the **three** correct options.

   A   Amount of oxygen

   B   Amount of light

   C   Amount of carbon dioxide

   D   Amount of chlorophyll

   E   Temperature

Temperature

2. Circle the correct option in the following sentence.

   The temperature at which enzymes controlling photosynthesis are destroyed is **25°C / 75°C / 14°C / 45°C**.

Carbon Dioxide Concentration

3. A plant is receiving plenty of light but its rate of photosynthesis stops increasing. What other factors might be responsible? Tick the correct option.

   A   Amount of carbon dioxide or the amount of oxygen

   B   Amount of carbon dioxide or the temperature

   C   Amount of chlorophyll or the temperature

   D   Amount of glucose or the amount of oxygen

Light Intensity

4. Explain why too little light can have a negative effect on a plant.

   ....

   ....

Artificial Controls

5. Fill in the missing words to complete the following sentence.

   To control the rate of photosynthesis, ... can be used to make plants grow

   more .... , becoming bigger and ....

Food Chains & Biomass

Food Chains

1 The text below represents a food chain.

Rosebush ➡ **Aphid** ➡ **Ladybird** ➡ **Blackbird**

Circle the correct options in the following sentences.

a) The producer in the food chain is the **aphid / blackbird / ladybird / rosebush**.

b) The herbivore in the food chain is the **aphid / blackbird / ladybird / rosebush**.

c) The top carnivore in the food chain is the **aphid / blackbird / ladybird / rosebush**.

2 Where does the initial source of energy for all food chains come from? Tick the correct option.

A The Moon ⬜

B The Sun ⬜

C The soil ⬜

D Animals ⬜

3 Briefly explain what biomass is.

....

....

Pyramid of Biomass

4 Energy is lost at all the stages in a food chain. What is the energy used for? Tick the **three** correct options.

A Photosynthesis ⬜

B Keeping warm ⬜

C Movement ⬜

D Growth ⬜

5 Give three ways in which the efficiency of a food chain can be improved.

a) ....

b) ....

c) ....

Recycling the Materials of Life

1 Fill in the missing words to complete the following sentences.

Organisms _____ material from the environment for _____

and other purposes. These materials are _____ to the environment when the

organisms _____ .

2 Give three factors that increase the rate at which microorganisms can digest materials.

a) _____ **b)** _____ **c)** _____

The Carbon Cycle

3 Using the diagram of the carbon cycle below, circle the correct options in the following sentences.

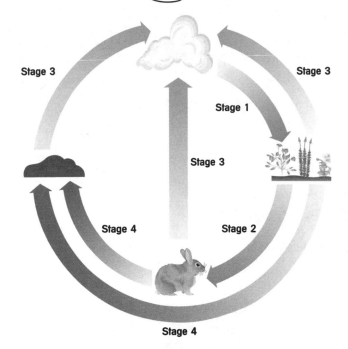

a) Stage 1 shows when **respiration / decomposition / photosynthesis / combustion** happens.

b) Stage 3 shows when **respiration / decomposition / photosynthesis / combustion** happens.

c) Stage 4 shows when **respiration / decomposition / photosynthesis / combustion** happens.

4 At stage 2, carbon is converted into certain substances in the animal. What are these substances?
Tick the correct option.

A Vitamins and minerals ◯   **B** Carbohydrates and proteins ◯

C Fats and fibre ◯   **D** Carbohydrates, fats and proteins ◯

Enzymes

Enzymes

1 Circle the correct options in the following sentences.

a) An enzyme is a **biological / chemical** catalyst that **speeds up / slows down** the rate of **biological / chemical** reactions in an organism.

b) Enzymes are made from **carbohydrate / fat / vitamin / protein** molecules. They are made up of long chains of **DNA / amino acids / fatty acids / starch molecules**.

2 Briefly explain what happens to an enzyme if the temperature goes too high.

....

....

Aerobic Respiration

3 **a)** What gas is used in aerobic respiration? Tick the correct option.

    A Carbon dioxide ◯   **B** Hydrogen ◯

    C Oxygen ◯   **D** Nitrogen ◯

b) What gas is produced during aerobic respiration? Tick the correct option.

    A Carbon dioxide ◯   **B** Hydrogen ◯

    C Oxygen ◯   **D** Nitrogen ◯

Enzymes Inside Living Cells

4 Give three processes in living cells that can be speeded up by enzymes.

a) ....

b) ....

c) ....

5 Choose the correct words from the options given to complete the following sentence.

amino acids   **muscles**   **molecules**   **proteins**   **temperature**

The energy released during respiration is used to build larger ...., enable

.... to contract, maintain a constant .... (in mammals

and birds) and to make .... in plants from ....

Enzymes Outside Living Cells

1 Specialised cells in glands in the digestive system produce digestive enzymes.

a) What type of enzyme breaks down fat? Tick the correct option.

A Protease ◯

B Carbohydrase ◯

C Cellulase ◯

D Lipase ◯

b) What type of enzyme breaks down protein? Tick the correct option.

A Protease ◯

B Carbohydrase ◯

C Cellulase ◯

D Lipase ◯

2 Which of the following organs produce digestive enzymes? Tick the **four** correct options.

A Rectum ◯

B Large intestine ◯

C Salivary glands ◯

D Stomach ◯

E Gall bladder ◯

F Pancreas ◯

G Small intestine ◯

H Liver ◯

3 a) What soluble product is produced by protease?

_____

b) What soluble product is produced by amylase?

_____

c) What two products are produced by lipase?

i) _____ **ii)** _____

Enzymes

Bile

1 The following questions are about bile.

   a) Which organ produces bile? ....

   b) Where is bile stored? ....

   c) Into what part of the body is bile released? ....

2 What are the jobs of bile? Tick the **two** correct options.

   A   To break down sugars   ◯

   B   To neutralise stomach acid   ◯

   C   To remove excess water   ◯

   D   To break down protein   ◯

   E   To emulsify fats   ◯

   F   To break down carbohydrates   ◯

Use of Enzymes

3 Which two enzymes might biological detergents contain? Tick the **two** correct options.

   A   Fat-digesting   ◯

   B   Glucose-digesting   ◯

   C   Bile-digesting   ◯

   D   Protein-digesting   ◯

4 Match statements **A**, **B**, **C** and **D** with the enzymes **1–4** listed below. Write the appropriate numbers in the boxes provided.

   1   Lipases   **2**   Carbohydrases

   3   Proteases   **4**   Isomerases

   A   Digest fat stains from clothes   ◯

   B   Used to produce fructose syrup used in slimming foods   ◯

   C   Pre-digest protein in baby foods   ◯

   D   Used to make chocolate and syrup   ◯

Controlling Body Conditions

Controlling Body Conditions

1 To function properly, what four things must the body control levels of?

a) ....

b) ....

c) ....

d) ....

Blood Glucose Concentration

2 What hormone is produced by the pancreas? Tick the correct option.

A ADH ◯

B Insulin ◯

C Glucose ◯

D Glycogen ◯

3 a) Apart from the pancreas, which other organ is involved in controlling blood sugar levels? Tick the correct option.

A Kidney ◯   B Liver ◯

C Brain ◯   D Heart ◯

b) What causes diabetes? Tick the correct option.

A Pancreas does not produce insulin ◯

B Liver does not produce glycogen ◯

C Kidneys do not remove glucose from the blood ◯

D Liver does not produce insulin ◯

Water and Ion Content

4 The body gains water and ions through food and drink. Fill in the missing words to complete the following sentences.

When the .... or .... content of the body is out of balance,

too much water may move in or out of the cells. This process is called .... ◻

Body Temperature

Body Temperature

1 a) Where are the receptors located that provide information about blood temperature? Tick the correct option.

   A Skin ◯   **B** Brain ◯

   C Kidneys ◯   **D** Lungs ◯

b) Circle the correct option in the following sentence.

The normal body temperature is **20°C / 100°C / 37°C / 75°C**.

HT

2 a) What changes occur if the body becomes too cold? Tick the **three** correct options.

   A Blood vessels in the skin dilate ◯

   B Sweat glands stop producing sweat ◯

   C Shivering occurs ◯

   D Skin becomes flushed ◯

   E Blood vessels in the skin constrict ◯

   F Heat loss increases ◯

b) Give two changes that occur if the body becomes too hot.

i) ....

ii) ....

Removing Waste Products

3 Choose the correct word from the options given to complete the following sentence.

amino acids   **glucose**   **urea**   **water**

The waste product removed by the kidneys is ....

4 Which of the following are waste products that need to be removed from the body in order to maintain a constant internal environment? Tick the **two** correct options.

   A Oxygen ◯   **B** Carbon dioxide ◯

   C Blood ◯   **D** Urea ◯

Chromosomes & Gametes

Human Body Cells

1 (Circle) the correct option in the following sentence.

Human body cells contain a total of **23 / 46 / 22 / 28** chromosomes.

2 a) What are sex cells known as? Tick the correct option.

A Genes ◯   **B** Alleles ◯

C Gametes ◯   **D** Chromosomes ◯

b) What do sex cells contain? Tick the correct option.

A Half the number of chromosomes as a normal body cell ◯

B The same number of chromosomes as a normal body cell ◯

C Twice the number of chromosomes as a normal body cell ◯

D Half the number of chromosomes of a sperm cell ◯

c) What is produced from the fusion of two sex cells?

....

Inheritance of the Sex Chromosome

3 a) Choose the correct chromosomes from the options given to complete the following sentence.

XY and YY   XX and XY   XX and YY   XF and XM

The sex chromosomes are ....

b) Which of the following are the female sex chromosomes, and which are the male sex chromosomes? Label them correctly.

i) ....   **ii)** ....

4 What determines the sex of an individual?

....

....

Cell Division

Mitosis

1 Mitosis is the division of body cells to make new cells.

a) When is mitosis not used in dividing cells? Tick the correct option.

A Asexual reproduction ⬭   **B** Gamete production ⬭

C Repair ⬭   **D** Growth ⬭

b) Fill in the missing words to complete the following sentences.

A copy of each _____ is made before a cell divides. The new cell has the same

_____ information as the _____ cell.

c) ⬭Circle the correct option in the following sentence.

When one cell has undergone mitosis, **1 / 2 / 4 / 8** 'daughter' cells will be made.

HT Meiosis

2 **a)** Choose the correct words from the options given to complete the following sentence.

ovaries   **chromosomes**   **eggs**

Meiosis takes place in the _____ and testes, and produces _____

and sperm containing 23 _____ .

b) What is the name of the four types of cell produced after meiosis?

_____

Fertilisation

3 During fertilisation the male and female sex cells join.

a) What does the new body cell contain?

_____

b) What happens to the new body cell next?

_____

Alleles

1 How many alleles does the gene controlling tongue-rolling ability have? Tick the correct option.

    A One ◯

    B Three ◯

    C Four ◯

    D Two ◯

2 Fill in the missing words to complete the following sentences.

    a) Where there are different alleles for a gene, one is known as the .... gene

    and the other is known as the .... gene.

    b) Using the correct genetic terms, describe the following alleles.

        i) BB ....

        ii) Bb ....

        iii) bb ....

3 Match definitions **A**, **B**, **C** and **D** with the keywords **1–4** listed below. Write the appropriate numbers in the boxes provided.

    1 Dominant   **2** Phenotype

    3 Heterozygous   **4** Homozygous

        A What the organism looks like   ◯

        B The stronger allele   ◯

        C Both alleles are the same   ◯

        D Different alleles   ◯

4 Fill in the missing words to complete the following sentences.

    a) A .... allele will control the characteristics of the gene if it's present on only one chromosome, or if it's present on both chromosomes.

    b) A .... allele will only control the characteristics of the gene if it's present on both chromosomes.

Genetic Diagrams

Monohybrid Inheritance

1 **a)** When is it useful to draw a genetic cross diagram?

to show trace of genes and which chromosomes are regressive and dominant

b) What does a genetic cross diagram show?

Inheritance of Eye Colour

2 **a)** John has blue eyes. Both his parents have brown eyes. His mother's genotype is Bb. What must John's father's genotype be? Tick the correct option.

A Bb ✓   **B** BB ◯   **C** bb ◯   **D** BBb ◯

b) Circle the correct option in the following sentence.

If both parents have blue eyes there is a **50% / 100% / 0% / 24%** chance that they will have a child with brown eyes.

HT

3 **a)** Complete this genetic diagram to show the possible genotypes of the offspring.

b) Complete the following sentence.

There is a _____ 50 _____ % chance that the offspring will have brown eyes.

Differentiation of Cells

4 Choose the correct words from the options given to complete the following sentence.

structure   **function**   **cells**

Differentiation is the result of _____ developing a specialised

_____ to carry out a specific _____ .

Chromosomes, DNA & Genes

Stem Cells

1 In which two places would you find stem cells?

a) *fetus*

b) *Bone marrow*

Chromosomes, DNA and Genes

2 What do the two strands of a DNA molecule coil together to form? Tick the correct option.

A Double spring ☐　　　　**B** Double twist ☐

C Double spiral ☐　　　　**D** Double helix ☑

HT

3 How do genes code for a particular characteristic?

Genetic Disorders

4 What is an inherited disease? Tick the correct option.

A A disease caused by microbes ☐

B A disease passed from person to person ☐

C A disease passed on from parent to child by genes ☐

D A self-inflicted disease ☐

5 Fill in the missing words to complete the following sentences.

a) Huntington's disease is a disorder of the ....

It's caused by a .... allele.

b) Cystic fibrosis is caused by a .... allele. It must be inherited from both

parents. The parents might not have the disorder, but they might be ....

Atoms

1. Choose the correct words from the options given to complete the following sentences.

   electrons   **protons**   **neutrons**

   a) An atom contains an equal number of .... and ....

   b) The nucleus contains .... and .... , and is surrounded

   by ....

2. Why do atoms have no charge? Tick the correct option.

   A   They contain the same number of electrons and protons

   B   They contain the same number of electrons and neutrons

   C   They contain the same number of protons and neutrons

   D   They contain the same number of protons, neutrons and electrons

3. Draw lines between the boxes to match each atomic particle to its charge.

Neutron		-1
Proton		0
Electron		+1

Electronic Configuration and Structure

4. The diagram shows the electron configuration of an atom.

   a) What is the proton (atomic) number of this atom?

   .... 8 ....

   b) What group does this atom belong to? .... 6 ....

   c) What period does this atom belong to? .... 2 ....

   d) What is the electron configuration of this atom?

   ....

   e) What would be the charge of an ion made from this atom? Tick the correct option.

   A -2 ✓   **B** -1 ○   **C** +1 ○   **D** +2 ○

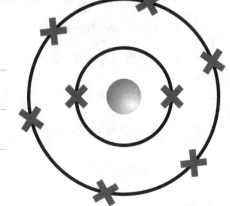

Alkali Metals & Halogens

The Alkali Metals (Group 1)

1 a) How many electrons does an alkali metal have in its outermost shell?

....

b) Fill in the missing words to complete the following sentence.

Alkali metals react with .... elements to form ....

compounds. The metal ion has a single .... charge.

The Halogens (Group 7)

2 Fill in the missing words to complete the following sentences.

a) A halogen has .... electrons in its outer shell.

b) Halogens react with .... metals to form .... compounds.

The halide ions have a single .... charge.

Mixtures and Compounds

3 a) Circle the correct options in the following sentences.

i) A **mixture / compound** consists of elements that are not chemically combined.

ii) The atoms of two or more elements in **mixtures / compounds** are chemically combined.

b) What happens to each atom when they form chemical bonds? Tick the correct option.

A They lose all electrons ⬭

B They get a full inner shell of electrons ⬭

C They become very big ⬭

D They get a full outer shell of electrons ⬭

HT Simple Molecular Compounds

4 Explain why simple molecules in gases, liquids and solids have relatively low boiling and melting points.

....

....

Ionic Bonding

Ionic Compounds

1 **a)** **i)** Do ionic compounds have high or low boiling points? ....

ii) Explain your answer to part i).

....

....

b) Why can ionic compounds conduct electricity when they are molten?

ions are free to move

The Ionic Bond

2 **a)** What is the definition of an ionic bond? Tick the correct option.

A A shared pair of electrons ☐

B Positive metal ions in a sea of electrons ☐

C Strong forces of attraction between oppositely charged ions ☐

D Weak forces of attraction between oppositely charged ions ☑

b) Circle the correct option in the following sentence.

An ion is **an atom** / ~~an element~~ / ~~a molecule~~ / **a charged atom**.

3 The diagram shows the electron configuration of an ionic compound.

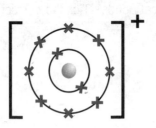 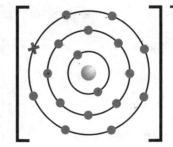

a) What is the name of this ionic compound?

sodium chloride

b) What is the formula of this ionic compound?

....

The Covalent Bond

1 a) Between what type(s) of atoms do covalent bonds form? Tick the correct option.

    A Metal and metal ◯

    B Metal and non-metal ◯

    C Non-metal and non-metal ✓

b) Which of the following is not an example of a covalently bonded compound? Tick the correct option.

    A Chlorine ◯   **B** Methane ◯

    C Water ◯   **D** Magnesium oxide ✓

2 Circle the correct options in the following sentences.

    a) The covalent bonds between atoms are **strong** / weak.

    b) The forces of attraction between molecules are **strong** / weak.

Covalent Bonding

3 a) Draw the electron configuration diagram for a hydrogen atom.

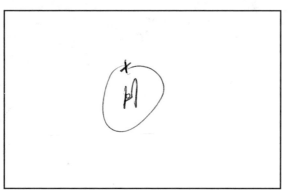

b) Draw the electron configuration diagram for a chlorine atom.

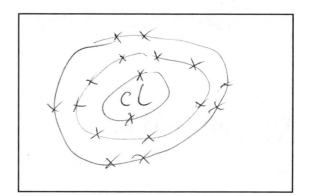

c) Draw the electron configuration diagram for a hydrogen chloride molecule.

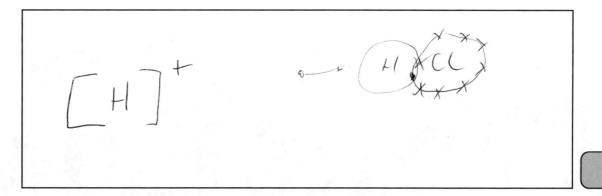

Covalent Structures

Giant Covalent Structures

1 The diagrams show two different forms of carbon.

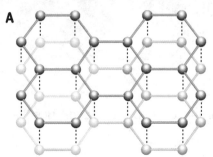

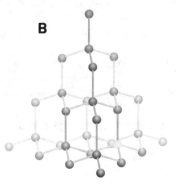

a) What are the names of the two forms of carbon shown?

A _Graphite_   B _Diamond_

b) Why is Form A soft? Tick the correct option.

A All of the atoms are held in a rigid 3-D structure

B There are delocalised electrons that are free to move between the layers

C The layers of carbon atoms can easily slide over each other ✓

D There are localised electrons that are not free to move in the layers of atoms

HT **c)** Why can Form B conduct electricity?

_____

Metals

2  the correct option in the following sentence.

Layers of **atoms** / **electrons** / **bonds** in metals are able to slide over each other, which makes metals easy to bend and shape.

HT

3 Explain how metals can conduct electricity.

_____

_____

Nanoparticles and Nanostructures

1 What is nanoscience?

....

2 Circle the correct options in the following sentences.

a) The symbol for a nanometre is **m / c / nm / mn**.

b) The structures studied in nanoscience are **1–10 / 10–100 / 1–100 / 1–1000** nanometres in size.

3 Is the following statement **true** or **false**?

The properties of nanoparticles are the same as the properties of the same materials in bulk.

....

4 Fill in the missing words to complete the following sentence.

Nanostructures can be .... to develop materials with new and

.... properties.

Nanocomposites

5 Give three advantages nanocomposites have over plastics.

a) ....

b) ....

c) ....

6 Give three ways in which nanotechnology is used in industry.

a) ....

b) ....

c) ....

7 What are smart materials?

....

....

The Periodic Table & Atoms

The Periodic Table

1 Fill in the missing words to complete the following sentence.

Whatever version of the periodic table is used, the _____ number is always the top

number and the _____ number is always at the bottom.

Mass Number and Atomic Number

2 Circle the correct options in the following sentences.

a) The mass number tells you the number of **protons / electrons** and neutrons in an atom.

b) The atomic number is the number of **protons / electrons / neutrons** in an atom.

3 How many protons does an oxygen atom have? Tick the correct option.

A 1 ◯   **B** 16 ◯

C 8 ◯   **D** 0 ◯

4 Which elements have six neutrons? Tick the **two** correct options.

A H ◯   **B** He ◯

C Li ◯   **D** Be ◯

E B ◯   **F** C ◯

G N ◯   **H** O ◯

5 a) What is the mass number of sodium?

_____

b) How many neutrons does a sodium atom have?

_____

6 Which of the statements below about the mass of particles in an atom is true? Tick the correct option.

A A proton has the same relative mass as a neutron ◯

B A proton has the same relative mass as an electron ◯

C A neutron has the same relative mass as an electron ◯

D A proton, a neutron and an electron all have the same relative mass ◯

Isotopes & Relative Formula Mass

Isotopes

1 What is an isotope? Tick the correct option.

A Atoms of the same element with the same number of protons and neutrons but a different number of electrons ◯

B Atoms of the same element with the same number of protons and electrons but a different number of neutrons ◯

C Atoms of the same element with the same number of electrons and neutrons but a different number of protons ◯

D Atoms of the same element with the same number of protons, neutrons and electrons ◯

Relative Atomic Mass, A_r

2 What is the relative atomic mass (A_r) of an element equal to? Tick the correct option.

A Its atomic mass ◯   **B** Its element symbol ◯

C Its mass number ◯   **D** Its electron number ◯

HT

3 a) What is the relative atomic mass of helium? _____ 4

b) Fill in the missing word to complete the following sentence.

The relative atomic mass is an average value for all the _____ of the element.

Relative Formula Mass, M_r

4 a) What does M_r stand for? Tick the correct option.

A The element manganese ◯

B The relative atomic mass ◯

C The mass number ◯

D The relative formula mass ◯

b) What is the M_r of iron oxide?

_____

_____

Percentage Mass

Calculating Percentage Mass

1. Write down the formula used to calculate percentage mass.

2. a) What is the percentage mass of calcium in calcium carbonate, $CaCO_3$? Tick the correct option. (You can use the space below to do your calculations.)

   A 40% ◯   B 100% ◯

   C 60% ◯   D 5% ◯

   b) What is the percentage mass of calcium in calcium oxide (CaO) to the nearest whole number?

HT Empirical Formula of a Compound

3. In an experiment, 2.24g of iron is burned in oxygen to make 3.2g of iron oxide.

   a) How much oxygen is used in this reaction?

   b) What is the empirical formula for iron oxide? Show your workings.

The Mole

1 Tick the **two** correct options to complete the following sentence. One mole of any substance…

   A will contain the same elements ☐

   B will contain the same number of particles ☐

   C is equal to the relative formula mass of a substance ☐

   D is equal to the relative atomic particle ☐

2 The following statements are about the molar mass of certain elements. Tick the **four** correct options. (You can use the periodic table to help you.)

   A The molar mass of hydrogen is 1g/mol ☐

   B The molar mass of sulfur is 32mol/g ☐

   C The molar mass of iodine is 124g/mol ☐

   D The molar mass of potassium is 39mol ☐

   E The molar mass of aluminium is 27g/mol ☐

   F The molar mass of zinc is 65mol/g ☐

   G The molar mass of oxygen is 16g/mol ☐

   H The molar mass of iron is 56g/mol ☐

3 **a)** Write the formula used to calculate the number of moles in a substance.

   b) Calculate the number of moles in 520g of calcium carbonate ($CaCO_3$).

   c) Calculate the mass of four moles of ammonia (NH_3).

Calculating Mass

HT Calculating the Mass of a Product

1 The equation for the chemical reaction that neutralises ammonia to produce ammonium nitrate is:

Ammonia + Nitric acid $\longrightarrow$ Ammonium nitrate

NH_3 + HNO_3 $\longrightarrow$ NH_4NO_3

a) Write down the relative atomic mass of each of the following elements.

    i) Nitrogen _____   **ii)** Hydrogen _____

b) What mass of ammonium nitrate can be produced from 10kg of ammonia? Tick the correct option.

    A 80kg ◯   **B** 47kg ◯

    C 17kg ◯   **D** 63kg ◯

c) What mass of ammonium nitrate can be produced from 252kg of nitric acid? Tick the correct option.

    A 68kg ◯   **B** 320kg ◯

    C 51kg ◯   **D** 63kg ◯

Calculating the Mass of a Reactant

2 Calcium carbonate and hydrochloric acid react together to produce calcium chloride, carbon dioxide and water. Below is the balanced symbol equation for this reaction.

$CaCO_3(s)$ + $2HCl(aq)$ $\longrightarrow$ $CaCl_2(aq)$ + $CO_2(g)$ + $H_2O(l)$

a) Work out the M_r for each of the reactants and products shown in the equation, and write them below.

    i) $CaCO_3$ _____   **ii)** $2HCl$ _____

    iii) $CaCl_2$ _____   **iv)** CO_2 _____

    v) H_2O _____

b) What is the total mass of all the reactants in the equation?

_____

c) What is the total mass of all the products in the equation?

_____

d) How much calcium carbonate is needed to produce 1kg (1000g) of calcium chloride?

_____

Yield & Atom Economy

Yield

1 Which of the following statements about chemical reactions is true? Tick the correct option.

    A Atoms are lost but never gained   ◯

    B Atoms are gained but never lost   ◯

    C Atoms are both lost and gained   ◯

    D Atoms are never lost or gained   ◯

2 a) What is a percentage yield? Tick the correct option.

    A The amount of reactant used   ◯

    B The amount of reactant used, compared with the product made   ◯

    C The actual amount of product made, compared with the amount of product that could have been made   ◯

    D The actual amount of reactant used, compared with the amount of reactant that could have been used   ◯

b) Write down the equation used for calculating percentage yield.

_____

_____

c) Fill in the missing number to complete the following sentence.

In an experiment Jamie made ethene from ethanol. He calculated that he could have made 10g of

ethene, but only collected 9g. His percentage yield is _____ %.

Calculating Atom Economy

3 Calcium carbonate can be thermally decomposed to make calcium oxide and carbon dioxide. Below is the symbol equation for this reaction:

$CaCO_3 \longrightarrow CaO + CO_2$

Fill in the missing value to complete the following sentence.

The atom economy of the thermal decomposition of calcium carbonate to make calcium oxide

is _____ %.

Reversible Reactions & the Haber Process

Reversible Reactions

1 What is a reversible reaction?

A reaction that can be reversed. products/
elements can be brought back.

The Haber Process

2 The diagram below shows a flow chart for the Haber process.

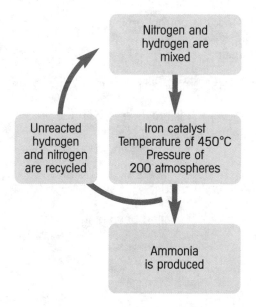

Nitrogen and hydrogen are mixed

Unreacted hydrogen and nitrogen are recycled

Iron catalyst
Temperature of 450°C
Pressure of 200 atmospheres

Ammonia is produced

a) Circle the correct option in the following sentence.

The product of this industrial process is **nitrogen / hydrogen / iron / ammonia**.

b) Which of the following are the correct equations for this industrial process?
Tick the **two** correct options.

A $N_2 + 3H_2 \rightleftharpoons 2NH_3$ ◯   **B** Nitrogen + Hydrogen $\rightleftharpoons$ Ammonia ◯

C Nitrogen + Iron $\rightleftharpoons$ Ammonia ◯   **D** $N_2 \rightleftharpoons 2NH_3 + 3H_2$ ◯

3 Why is the Haber Process carried out at about 400°C? Tick the correct option.

A To maximise reaction rate ◯

B To maximise yield ◯

C To compromise between reaction rate and yield ◯

D It has always been done at this temperature ◯

Rates of Reactions

1 Fill in the missing word to complete the following sentence.

_____ energy is the name given to the minimum amount of energy required to cause a chemical reaction.

Temperature

2 Collision theory can be used to explain the rates of chemical reactions.

Why does heating a reaction increase the rate of reaction? Tick the **three** correct options.

A The particles have more energy ◯

B The particles are more likely to hit each other ◯

C Each collision is more likely to form a product ◯

D There are more reactant particles ◯

E There are more reactant particles exposed ◯

Concentration

3 Circle the correct options in the following sentences.

a) In a **low / high** concentration reaction, the particles are **close together / spread out**. They collide less often, so there are **fewer / more** successful collisions.

b) In a **low / high** concentration reaction, the particles are **close together / spread out**. They collide more often, so there are **fewer / more** successful collisions.

c) **Increasing / decreasing** the pressure of reacting gases also increases the frequency of collisions.

HT

4 What is the unit of concentration for liquids? Tick the correct option(s).

A Moles per cubic decimetre ◯

B Mol/dm^3 ◯

C Mol/dm ◯

D Miles per square decimetre ◯

5 Circle the correct option in the following sentence.

Equal volumes of gases at the same temperature and pressure contain **different / equal** numbers of molecules.

Chemical Reactions

Surface Area

1 Explain why increasing the surface area of pieces of a solid reactant also increases the rate of reaction.

smaller particle will react faster

Using a Catalyst

2 Fill in the missing words to complete the following sentences.

A catalyst is a _____ that changes the _____ of a chemical

reaction. It's not _____ during the reaction.

Analysing the Rate of Reaction

3 Shaheen decided to investigate the effect of changing the concentration of acid on the rate of reaction with a metal carbonate.

How could Shaheen monitor the rate of reaction? Tick the **two** correct options.

A Collect the gas ◯   **B** Disappearing cross ◯   **C** Monitor the mass ◯

Plotting Reaction Rates

4 The amount of a reactant can be monitored as a reaction progresses. This data can then be used to plot a graph and the rate of reaction can be calculated.

Look carefully at the following graphs to help you answer questions a) and b).

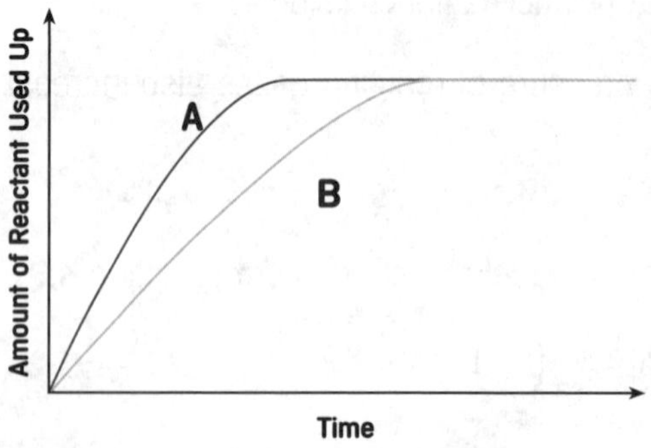

a) What could cause the reactions to stop? Tick the correct option.

A One of the reactants being used up ◯   **B** The products being removed ◯

C The temperature being too low ◯   **D** The pressure being too low ◯

b) Fill in the missing letter to complete the following sentence.

The line that shows the fastest rate of reaction is _____ .

Exothermic & Endothermic Reactions

Chemical Reactions

1 A new product and an energy change always accompany chemical reactions.

How is energy normally transferred in a chemical reaction? Tick the correct option.

A Kinetic energy ⬜   **B** Potential energy ⬜

C Thermal energy ⬜   **D** Sound energy ⬜

Exothermic Reactions

2 Fill in the missing words to complete the following sentence.

Three examples of exothermic reactions are .... , ... and

....

Endothermic Reactions

3 Which of the following statements are true for an endothermic reaction? Tick the **three** correct options.

A Reactants have more energy than products ⬜

B Products have more energy than reactants ⬜

C Energy is taken in from the surroundings ⬜

D Energy is released to the surroundings ⬜

E Activation energy is needed to make a reaction happen ⬜

HT Changing Reaction Conditions

4 Which of the following statements about exothermic reactions are true? Tick the **three** correct options.

A They are accompanied by a temperature rise ⬜

B If the temperature is raised the yield increases ⬜

C If the temperature is lowered the yield increases ⬜

D If the temperature is raised the yield decreases ⬜

E They are accompanied by a fall in temperature ⬜

5 Circle the correct option in the following sentence.

In gaseous reactions an increase in pressure favours the reaction that produces the
least / greatest number of molecules.

Reversible Reactions

Reversible Reactions

1 Ammonia and a gas can be made when solid ammonium chloride undergoes thermal decomposition. This is a reversible reaction. Write down a word equation for this reaction.

....

....

2 Look carefully at the diagram. What type of forward reaction has occurred? Tick the **three** correct options.

A Irreversible ◯

B Reversible ◯

C Chemical ◯

D Physical ◯

E Exothermic ◯

F Endothermic ◯

Sustainable Development

3 Give two reasons why it's important to minimise energy use and waste in an industrial process.

a) ....

b) ....

4 Which of the following is true about non-vigorous reactions? Tick the **three** correct options.

A Less energy is used ◯

B The cost is greater ◯

C There is a less efficient reaction ◯

D More energy is released into the environment ◯

E Less energy is released into the environment ◯

F There is a more efficient reaction ◯

Reversible Reactions & Closed Systems

HT Reversible Reactions

1 The Haber process is an important industrial process used to make ammonia (NH_3) from hydrogen (H_2) and nitrogen (N_2).

a) Why is the Haber process run at about 200 atmospheres? Tick the correct option.

A   To maximise rate ⬭

B   To maximise yield ⬭

C   To compromise between rate and yield ⬭

D   It has always been done at this pressure ⬭

b) Look carefully at the table. What conclusion about temperature can you draw from this data? Tick the correct option.

Pressure (atmospheres)	Percentage Yield of Ammonia at 300°C	Percentage Yield of Ammonia at 600°C
100	43	4
200	62	12
300	74	18
400	79	19

A   As temperature increases, yield increases ⬭

B   As temperature increases, there is no change in yield ⬭

C   As temperature increases, yield decreases ⬭

D   As temperature increases, pressure decreases ⬭

Closed Systems

2 **a)** Circle the correct options in the following sentences.

The Haber process is a reversible, **exothermic / endothermic / physical / chemical** reaction. It's exothermic in the forward direction. This means that it's **exothermic / endothermic / physical / chemical** in the reverse direction. An equilibrium is achieved when the forward rate is **greater than / smaller than / equal to** the reverse rate. This can only happen in a **dynamic / equilibrium / closed** system.

b) If a reversible reaction is carried out in a closed system, explain what happens when equilibrium is reached.

Electrolysis

State Symbols

1 Circle the correct options in the following sentence.

To undergo electrolysis, ionic compounds must be **(s) / (l)** or **(g) / (aq)**.

Electrolysis

2 Write down a definition of electrolysis.

....

....

Redox Reactions

3 **a)** What two chemical events must occur to form a redox reaction?

i) .... **ii)** ....

b) Circle the correct options in the following sentences.

In the electrolysis of molten zinc chloride, zinc **ions / atoms** are **oxidised / reduced** to zinc **ions / atoms** at the negative electrode. At the positive electrode, negatively charged ions are **oxidised / reduced**.

Electrolysis of Sodium Chloride Solution

4 Sodium chloride is an ionic compound that can undergo electrolysis.

Look carefully at the diagram. What is produced at the positive electrode? Tick the correct option.

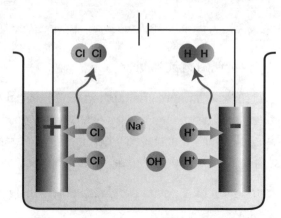

A Chlorine ⬜ **B** Hydrogen ⬜

C Sodium ⬜ **D** Sodium hydroxide ⬜

Electrolysis

Purification of Copper by Electrolysis

1 a) In the purification of copper what is the positive electrode made from? Tick the correct option.

    A Impure copper ⬭   **B** Pure copper ⬭

    C Carbon ⬭   **D** Any of the above ⬭

b) i) What is formed at the negative electrode?

....

   ii) Explain how your answer to part i) forms.

....

....

(HT) Electrolysis Equations

2 The diagram shows the electrolysis of sodium chloride.

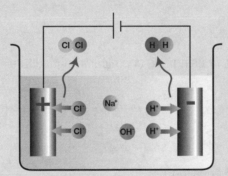

Complete the following half-equation for the reaction at the negative electrode.

$2H^+(aq) + 2e^- \longrightarrow$ ....

Indicators and pH Scale

3 Fill in the missing words to complete the following sentences.

a) Indicators are dyes that change colour according to whether the solutions they are in are

.... or ....

b) The .... scale measures the acidity or .... of

an .... solution.

Neutralisation

Neutralisation

1 When an _____ and an _____ are added together in the correct amounts they 'cancel out' each other. This type of reaction is called neutralisation.

2 Circle the correct option in the following sentence.

The pH of a neutral chemical is **1 / 4 / 7 / 14**.

3 What is the equation for neutralisation? Tick the correct option.

A $H_2O(aq) \longrightarrow H^+(aq) + OH^-(aq)$ ⬭   B $H_2O(l) \longrightarrow H^+(aq) + OH^-(aq)$ ⬭

C $H^+(aq) + OH^-(aq) \longrightarrow H_2O(l)$ ⬭   D $H^+(aq) + OH^-(aq) \longrightarrow H_2O(aq)$ ⬭

Neutralising Ammonia

4 a) When ammonia neutralises nitric acid, what product is formed?

_____

b) Give an example of how this chemical can benefit agriculture.

_____

c) Explain the potential dangers of using this chemical in agriculture.

_____

_____

5 Complete the following chemical equation.

$NH_3(aq) + HNO_3(aq) \longrightarrow$ _____ .

6 a) Fill in the missing words to complete the following sentence.

Ammonia can be neutralised with _____ to form ammonium

_____ .

b) Complete the table to show the products formed when ammonium hydroxide is neutralised with different acids.

	Hydrochloric Acid	Sulfuric Acid	Nitric Acid
Ammonium Hydroxide	i) _____ + water	ii) _____ + water	iii) _____ + water

Forming Salts

Soluble Salts from Metals

1 What is a salt?

....

....

2 Which of the following metals reacts most violently with acid? Tick the correct option.

A Silver ◯   **B** Magnesium ◯   **C** Zinc ◯   **D** Potassium ◯

Soluble Salts from Insoluble Bases

3 Fill in the missing words to complete the following sentences.

a) .... are the oxides and hydroxides of metals.

b) Soluble bases are called ....

4 Complete the word equation to show the general reaction that produces soluble salts from insoluble bases.

Acid + Base ➡ .... + Water

Salts of Alkali Metals

5 Briefly explain how salts of alkali metals can be made.

....

....

6 What salt is produced when sodium hydroxide is reacted with nitric acid?

....

Insoluble Salts

7 Fill in the missing words to complete the following sentences.

a) Insoluble salts are made by mixing appropriate solutions of .... to

form a ....

b) Magnesium .... are precipitated out as magnesium

....

◻

Speed

Speed

1 What two measurements must you take to calculate the speed of an object? Tick the correct option.

A Distance and direction of travel ☐   **B** Time and direction of travel ☐

C Distance and time   **D** Acceleration and direction of travel ☐

2 You can calculate speed using the formula:

$$\text{Speed (m/s)} = \frac{\text{Distance travelled (m)}}{\text{Time taken (s)}}$$

Jill ran 1500m in 5 minutes and 20 seconds. What was Jill's average speed?

$$\frac{1500}{5.2}$$

Distance–Time Graphs

3 a) The graph shows the journey of a runner. Fill in the missing values to complete the following sentences.

In 30 minutes he runs _____ km.

After travelling _____ km he

rests for _____ minutes.

b) What was the runner's speed in km/h for the first 15 minutes? Tick the correct option.

A 12km/h ☐

B 0.2km/h ☐

C 10km/h ☐

D 3km/h ☐

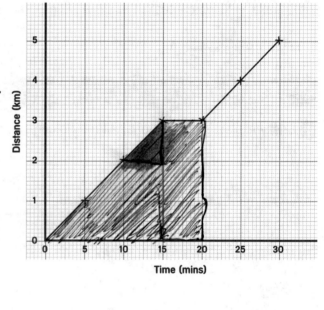

Velocity

4 Explain the difference between velocity and speed.

_____

_____

Acceleration

1 (Circle) the correct options in the following sentences.

a) Acceleration is the rate of change of an object's **distance / time / velocity / direction**.

b) To work out the acceleration of a moving object, you need to know the change in **distance / time / velocity / direction** and the **time taken / direction / distance travelled** for this change to occur.

2 What is the formula used to calculate acceleration? You should specify the unit of measure for each variable.

Velocity–Time Graphs

3 a) Look at the four graphs. Which graph shows an object accelerating at 3m/s²? Tick the correct option.

   A Graph 1 ◯

   B Graph 2 ◯

   C Graph 3 ✓

   D Graph 4 ◯

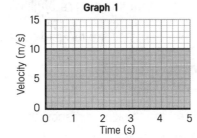

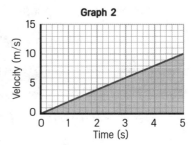

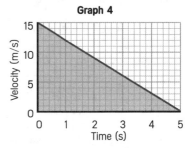

b) What does the area under a velocity–time graph show? Tick the correct option.

   A The average velocity of the object during its journey ◯

   B The total distance travelled by the object during its journey ◯

   C The average acceleration of the object during its journey ◯

   D The total time for the journey ◯

c) (Circle) the correct option in the following sentence.

The total distance travelled by the object in Graph 1 is **5m / 10m / 15m / 50m**.

Forces

Forces

1 Fill in the missing words to complete the following sentences.

Forces are pushes or _pulls_. They are measured in _Newtons_ and

may vary in size and act in different _____.

Friction

2 James is riding his jet ski at a constant speed of 15m/s. The jet ski's engines provide a forward force. Is there a force acting in the opposite direction? Tick the correct option.

A Yes, the jet ski's weight opposes the force from the engines

B Yes, upthrust opposes the force from the jet ski's engines

C Yes, friction opposes the force from the jet ski's engines

D No, the jet ski is travelling forwards so the forward force must be unbalanced

Stopping Distance

3 The stopping distance is the sum of the thinking distance and the braking distance. Which of the following factors would increase the **thinking** distance? Tick the **two** correct options.

A A vehicle that is well-maintained

B A vehicle that is travelling fast

C Good visibility

D An icy road

E A driver who is tired

F A driver who is under the influence of alcohol

How Forces Affect Movement

4 A hawk is flying with a constant velocity. However, if an unbalanced force acts on the hawk, its velocity will change. What noticeable effect might this have? Tick the **three** correct options.

A The hawk might speed up

B The hawk might slow down

C The hawk might continue flying at a constant speed, in a straight line

D The hawk might continue flying at a constant speed, but change direction

E The hawk's weight might increase

F The hawk's weight might decrease

Force, Mass & Acceleration

Force, Mass and Acceleration

1 A hockey player hits a puck with a small force, making it accelerate. Circle the correct options in the following sentences.

    a) A puck that's hit with a bigger force will experience **a smaller / the same / a greater** acceleration.

    b) A puck with a greater mass that's hit with the same force will experience **a smaller / the same / a greater** acceleration.

2 What is the formula that describes the relationship between force, mass and acceleration? You should state the unit of measure for each variable.

3 What is a newton (N)?

4 A car is moving at a constant speed of 30m/s. The total mass of the car and the driver is 1000kg.

    a) If the driving force is 3000N, what is the value of the frictional force?

    b) If the driver increases the driving force to 4000N, what is the acceleration of the car?

5 A motorcycle is moving along a straight road. The total mass of the motorcyclist and the bike is 250kg. The motorcycle accelerates at 2m/s². Calculate the force needed to produce this acceleration.

6 Will the car or the lorry have the greatest acceleration? Explain your answer.

2500N   5000N   2500N   5000N

1000kg   2000kg

Terminal Velocity

Terminal Velocity

1 What is meant by the term 'terminal velocity'?

....

....

2 **a)** The graph shows the velocity of a skydiver against time.

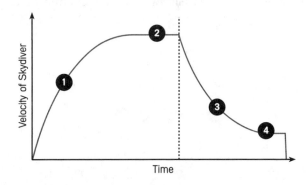

Match statements **A**, **B**, **C** and **D** with the labels **1–4** on the graph. Write the appropriate numbers in the boxes provided.

A   The skydiver's speed is decreasing

B   The skydiver's parachute is open and his speed is constant

C   The skydiver's speed is constant. He has not yet opened his parachute

D   The skydiver's speed is increasing

b) Circle the correct options in the following sentences.

i)   A skydiver jumps from a helicopter, which is hovering high above the ground. At the instant he jumps **his mass / his weight / air resistance** is equal to zero, so **his mass / his weight / air resistance** causes him to accelerate downwards.

ii) As he accelerates downwards, the upward force of **his mass / his weight / air resistance** gradually increases.

iii) The skydiver reaches a constant speed when the upward force is **smaller than / equal to / greater than** the downward force. At this point the skydiver has reached his **ultimate velocity / top velocity / terminal velocity**.

3 After a few minutes of freefall, the downward force acting on a skydiver is 600N. The upward force of air resistance is also 600N. What is the resultant force acting on the skydiver?

....

Work & Kinetic Energy

Work

1 When Matilda rolls a ball to Pablo, work is done on the ball. What does this mean? Tick the correct option.

    A   The ball heats up slightly (due to friction) as it rolls ☑

    B   Matilda accelerates the ball ☑

    C   Matilda exerts a force on the ball ☑

    D   Matilda transfers energy to the ball ☑

2 An elephant is being transported between zoos. A crane is used to lift with a force equal to the elephant's weight: 20kN. It lifts the elephant a vertical distance of 6 metres. Complete the following sentence.

The crane has done _____ kJ of work on the elephant.

3 Which of the devices below can store elastic potential energy? Tick the **three** correct options.

A A wind-up toy train ◯		**B** A petrol tank	◯
C A sling-shot ◯		**D** A bungee cord	◯
E A battery ◯		**F** A grandfather clock, powered by falling weights	◯

Kinetic Energy

4 a) What is kinetic energy?

energy formed whilst moving (from movement)

b) A greyhound runs at a constant speed of 20m/s. What happens to its kinetic energy? Tick the correct option.

    A   It has no kinetic energy ◯

    B   Its kinetic energy decreases, due to friction ◯

    C   As it runs for longer, its kinetic energy increases ◯

    D   Its speed isn't changing, so its kinetic energy doesn't change ◯

HT

5 Racing horses, greyhounds and hares can all reach speeds of around 20m/s. Of the three, the horse has the biggest mass and the hare has the smallest mass. If all three animals are running at 20m/s, which will have the least kinetic energy?

_____

Momentum

Momentum

1 a) What is momentum?

_____

_____

b) What two things does momentum depend on?

i) _____

ii) _____

2 Write down the equation for calculating momentum.

_____

3 A jogger has a mass of 80kg and is running at a velocity of 0.4m/s. What is the jogger's momentum? Tick the correct option. (You can use the line below for your calculations.)

A 320kg m/s ⬭   **B** 200kg m/s ⬭

C 20kg m/s ⬭   **D** 32kg m/s ⬭

_____

4 A truck is moving with a velocity of 18m/s. Calculate its mass if it has a momentum of 61 000kg m/s.

_____

_____

Magnitude and Direction

5 A tennis ball has a mass of 0.06kg. When it's served, it moves away from the racket with a velocity of 30m/s. Circle the correct options in the following sentences.

a) The momentum of the ball after the serve is **0.6 / 1.2 / 1.8 / 3.0** kg m/s.

b) The ball is returned by the other player at a velocity of -25m/s. On its return, the momentum of the ball is **-0.6 / -0.9 / -1.2 / -1.5** kg m/s.

6 A car of mass 1200kg is travelling at a velocity of 15m/s. What happens to its velocity and its momentum if the car then travels in the opposite direction with a speed of 15m/s?

_____

_____

Momentum

Force and Change in Momentum

1 Why does spreading out the change of momentum over a longer time reduce the risk of injury to a driver in a car crash? Tick the correct option.

A It gives the driver time to react ⬭

B It reduces the maximum force on the driver ⬭

C It enables the driver to steer away from the collision ⬭

D It reduces the velocity of the car ⬭

HT

2 Fill in the missing values to complete the following sentences.

In a crash-test laboratory, a dummy of mass 70kg hit a wall at a velocity of 20m/s. The dummy had a

momentum of .... The dummy was brought to rest (zero velocity) in 1.4 seconds.

The change of momentum of the dummy was .... The average force exerted on

the dummy was ....

3 Use ideas of momentum and force to explain why airbags reduce the level of injury in a car crash.

....

....

4 a) Vicki kicked a stationary ball of mass 0.5kg with a force of 20N whilst her foot remained in contact with the ball for 0.15s. Fill in the missing values to complete the following sentence.

The ball left Vicki's foot with a momentum of .... kg m/s and a velocity of

.... m/s.

b) Leila is a better football player than Vicki and when she kicked the same ball with the same force her foot remained in contact with the ball for 0.3s. Fill in the missing values to complete the following sentence.

The ball left Leila's foot with a momentum of .... kg m/s and a velocity of

.... m/s. ⬭

Collisions & Explosions

Collisions and Explosions

1 a) Collisions and explosions follow the law of conservation of momentum. What does conservation of momentum mean? Tick the correct option.

A Momentum never changes ◯

B Collisions are the same as backwards explosions ◯

C The momentum of each object before a collision or explosion is the same as the momentum of each object after the collision or explosion ◯

D The total momentum of the objects involved in a collision or explosion is the same before the event as after the event ◯

b) Look carefully at the image. In this question the momentum of each car is positive.

Before

Car A   20m/s   Car B   9m/s

1200kg   1000kg

After

2200kg

Circle the correct options in the following sentences.

i) Before the collision, Car A has a momentum of **24 000 / 9000 / 1200 / 25 000** kg m/s and Car B has a momentum of **19 000 / 2000 / 9000 / 25 000** kg m/s. The total momentum before the collision is **15 000 / 11 000 / 25 000 / 33 000** kg m/s.

ii) After the collision, the two cars move off together. Their total momentum is **15 000 / 11 000 / 25 000 / 33 000** kg m/s and they have a combined mass of 2200kg. They will move off with a velocity of **12 / 15 / 18 / 21** m/s.

2 Ali was standing on a skateboard, which wasn't moving. He caught a very heavy sports ball, which was thrown straight at him with a velocity of 18m/s. He didn't fall off the skateboard. What happened next? Tick the correct option.

A Ali and the skateboard remained still ◯

B Ali, the skateboard and the ball moved with a velocity of 18m/s ◯

C Ali, the skateboard and the ball moved with a velocity of less than 18m/s ◯

D Ali, the skateboard and the ball moved with a velocity of more than 18m/s ◯

3 Circle the correct option in the following sentence.

A cricket ball is thrown at 30m/s. Its momentum is 4.8kg m/s, so the mass of the ball is **0.12 / 0.16 / 0.20 / 0.24** kg.

Static Electricity

1 When a Perspex rod is rubbed with a cloth the rod becomes positively charged. Why is this?
Tick the correct option.

A The rod has gained protons ◯   **B** The rod has lost electrons ◯

C The cloth has lost protons ◯   **D** The rod has gained protons and lost electrons ◯

Repulsion and Attraction

2 Circle the correct options in the following sentences.

a) Materials with the same charge **attract / repel** each other.

b) Materials with different charges **attract / repel** each other.

The Uses of Static

3 Give two examples of devices that use electrostatic charges.

a) ....

b) ....

Electrostatic Smoke Precipitator

4 The diagram shows a cross-section of an electrostatic smoke precipitator.

Match statements **A, B, C** and **D**, with the labels **1–4** on the diagram.

Write the appropriate number in the boxes provided.

A Positively charged particles collect at negative plates at the side of the chimney ◯

B Positively charged particles repel each other towards the sides of the chimney ◯

C Smoke and waste gases ◯

D Positive grid charges particles as they pass through ◯

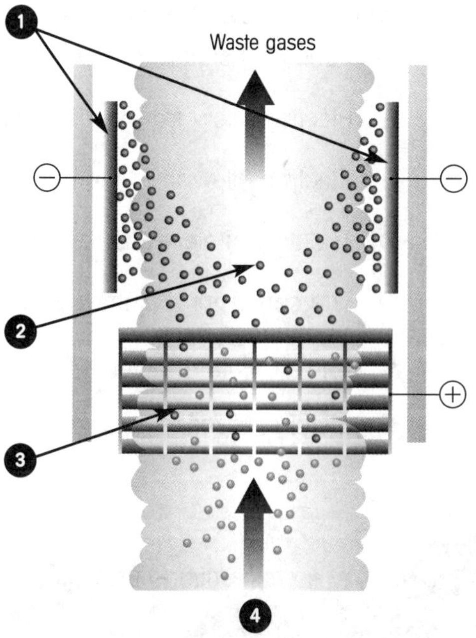

Waste gases

Static Electricity

The Photocopier

1 The following statements describe how a photocopier works. They are in the wrong order. Number the statements **1–6** to show the correct order.

A Charged impression on the plate attracts tiny specs of black powder ◯

B Paper is heated to fix the final image ◯

C Copying plate is electrically charged ◯

D Powder is transferred from the plate to the paper ◯

E Image of the page to be copied is projected onto the plate ◯

F Charge leaks away due to light, leaving an electrostatic impression of the page ◯

2 Does the electrically charged plate in a photocopier usually carry a positive or negative charge?

Discharge of Static Electricity

3 Briefly describe what is meant by 'discharging static electricity'.

4 Which of the following statements describe what happens when a conductor touches a negatively charged dome? Tick the **three** correct options.

A Electrons flow from earth to the dome ◯

B Electrons flow from the dome to earth ◯

C The flow of electrons is an electric current ◯

D The conductor becomes permanently charged ◯

E Rubber strips make good conductors ◯

F Metal rods make good conductors ◯

HT

5 Circle the correct options in the following sentence.

If the potential difference between an object and a nearby, earthed conductor rises high enough, the surrounding air molecules **are destroyed / become ionised / disappear** and there's a **fusion / chemical reaction / spark** as **recharge / discharge / uncharge** occurs. ◯

Circuits

1 Which of the following statements about electric circuits are true? Tick the **two** correct options.

    A   An ammeter measures the current of the circuit   ○

    B   A voltmeter measures the current of the circuit   ○

    C   An electric current flows if there's a potential difference across the ends of a component   ○

    D   An ammeter measures the resistance of the circuit   ○

2 a) Circuit 1 contains 1 battery and 1 lamp. Circuit 2 contains 1 battery and 2 lamps.
Compared to circuit 1, how brightly will the lamps in circuit 2 light up? Tick the correct option.

    A   The same brightness   ○

    B   Brighter   ○

    C   Less bright   ○

    D   You can't tell   ○

b) Circuit 3 contains 2 batteries and 2 lamps. Compared to circuit 1, how brightly will the lamps in circuit 3 light up? Tick the correct option.

    A   The same brightness   ○

    B   Brighter   ○

    C   Less bright   ○

    D   You can't tell   ○

3 Which of the following factors determine the amount of current that flows through a component?
Tick the **two** correct options.

    A   The thickness of the wires used in the circuit   ○

    B   The potential difference across the component   ○

    C   Whether a voltmeter is connected or not   ○

    D   The resistance of the component   ○

    E   The length of the wires used in the circuit   ○

    F   The distance between the component and the power source   ○

4 Fill in the missing word(s) to complete the following sentence.

The greater the resistance of a component, the greater the _____

needed to maintain a particular current.

Electric Circuits

Resistance

1 Briefly explain what resistance in a circuit is.

2 What is the formula that you would use to calculate potential difference?

$$V = IR \qquad voltage = current \times resistance$$

3 A circuit has a potential difference of 6V and a current of 3A. What is the resistance?

$2\,\Omega$

Resistors

4 Below are three current–voltage graphs.

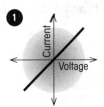 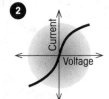 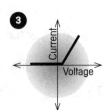

Which graph corresponds to each of the following components? Enter the appropriate numbers in the boxes provided.

A A diode ☐

B A resistor at a constant temperature ☐

C A filament lamp ☐

5 Match statements **A, B, C** and **D** with the resistors **1–4** listed below. Write the appropriate numbers in the boxes provided.

1 Light dependent resistor **2** Thermistor

3 Diode **4** Filament lamp

A Resistance decreases as the temperature of the resistor increases ☐

B Resistance increases as the temperature of the resistor increases ☐

C Resistance decreases as light intensity increases ☐

D The resistor has a very high resistance in one direction ☐

Series and Parallel Circuits

1 Fill in the missing words to complete the following sentences.

a) A circuit in which all the components are connected separately in their own loop, going from one end

of the battery to the other, is called a _____ circuit.

b) A circuit in which all the components are connected one after the other in a single loop is called a

_____ circuit.

2 Which of the following statements best describes the current in a parallel circuit? Tick the correct option.

A The total current is the product of the current through the separate components ⬭

B The same current flows through each component ⬭

C The current decreases each time it passes through a component ⬭

D The total current is equal to the sum of the currents through the separate components ⬭

3 Which of the following statements best describes what happens to the potential difference in a series circuit? Tick the correct option.

A The potential difference across each component is the same ⬭

B The potential difference is divided up between the components ⬭

C The potential difference increases as more components are added ⬭

D The potential difference is equal to the current ⬭

4 The diagram shows a parallel circuit. Each cell provides a potential difference of 1.5V.

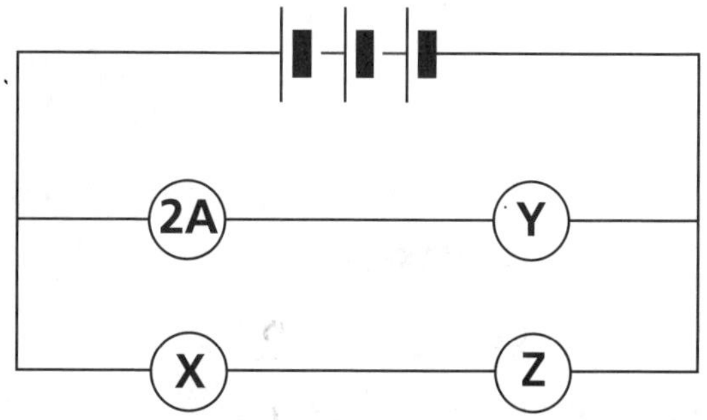

a) What is the value of the current at point X?

_____

b) What is the value of the potential difference at point Y?

_____

c) What is the value of the potential difference at point Z?

_____

Connecting Cells in Series

5 Circle the correct option in the following sentence.

Four 1.5V cells are connected in series, creating a total potential difference of **1.5V / 3V / 5.5V / 6V**.

⬭

Currents

Currents

1 (Circle) the correct option in the following sentence.

The approximate voltage of UK mains electricity is **100V / 230V / 60V / 550V**.

2 Fill in the missing words to complete the following sentences.

a) An _____ circuit changes the direction of current flow back and forth

continuously. A _____ current flows in the same direction.

b) Briefly explain what the 'frequency' of a current is.

_____

_____

The Three-Pin Plug

3 The diagram below shows a three-pin plug.

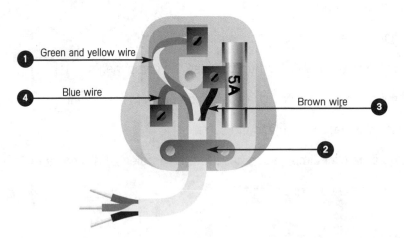

Match statements **A**, **B**, **C** and **D** with the labels **1–4** on the diagram. Write the appropriate numbers in the boxes provided.

A Cable grip ②

B Earth wire ①

C Neutral wire ④

D Live wire ③

4 What material is used to make the pins of a plug? Briefly explain why it's used.

_____

Circuit Breakers and Fuses

1 What is the purpose of a circuit breaker or fuse?

_____

_____

2 What is one advantage of circuit breakers over conventional fuses? Tick the correct option.

A They can be reset ⬜

B They last longer than fuses ⬜

C They are cheaper than fuses ⬜

D They are more reliable than fuses ⬜

3 Briefly explain how a fuse works.

_____

_____

Earthing

4 The steps **A, B, C, D** and **E** describe how a fuse protects a poorly wired appliance from damage. They are in the wrong order. Number the steps **1–5** to show the correct order.

A Large current flows to earth ⬜

B Live wire touches earthed metal casing ⬜

C Live current falls to zero ⬜

D Current in live wire increases ⬜

E Fuse melts ⬜

5 What two things protect the appliance and user? Tick the **two** correct options.

A The plug ⬜

B The earth wire ⬜

C The cabling ⬜

D The fuse ⬜

Power

Power

1 Which two sets of measurements could you use to calculate the power of an appliance? Tick the **two** correct options.

A   Potential difference and time ☐

B   Energy transformed and time ☐

C   Energy transformed and current ☐

D   Potential difference and current ☐

E   Current and time ☐

F   Charge and time ☐

2 An electric motor works at a current of 3A and a potential difference of 24V. What is the power of the motor?

HT Charge

3 **a)** Circle the correct option in the following sentence.

The unit of charge is the **joule / volt / ampere / coulomb**.

b) A 0.5 amp circuit is switched on for 60 seconds. What is the charge?

Transforming Energy

4 A simple series circuit contains a switch, a lamp and an ammeter. There is a 6V power supply. When the lamp is switched on for 5 minutes the reading on the ammeter is 3A.

Fill in the missing values to complete the following sentences. Don't forget to specify the units of measure.

a) The charge that flows through the circuit is ....

b) The power of the lamp is ....

c) The energy transformed is ....

5 Fill in the missing word to complete the following sentence.

The .... the potential difference, the more energy transformed per coulomb. ☐

Atoms & Radiation

Atoms

1 Which of the following particles can't be found in an atom? Tick the correct option.

    A   Proton   ◯

    B   Neutron   ◯

    C   Ion   ◯

    D   Electron   ◯

2 Explain why an atom as a whole doesn't have an electrical charge.

_____

3 What are isotopes?

_____

Radioactive Decay

4 Which of the following statements about radioactivity are true? Tick the **three** correct options.

    A   Radioactive materials have unstable nuclei   ◯

    B   Alpha radiation is a form of radioactive decay   ◯

    C   Radioactive materials become more radioactive as time passes   ◯

    D   Radioactive atoms have stable nuclei   ◯

    E   A gamma particle is a fast-moving electron   ◯

    F   Radioactive isotopes may disintegrate and emit radiation   ◯

Alpha Decay

5 **a)**   Fill in the missing word to complete the following sentence.

    An alpha particle can also be described as a(n) _____ .

    b)   An alpha particle is made up of four smaller particles. What are these four particles? Tick the correct option.

        A   Three protons and one neutron   ◯

        B   Four protons   ◯

        C   Two protons and two electrons   ◯

        D   Two protons and two neutrons   ◯

Radiation

Beta Decay

1 Which of the following statements about beta decay are true? Tick the **three** correct options.

    A A beta particle is like an alpha particle ⬭

    B A beta particle is a helium nucleus ⬭

    C A beta particle is formed when a neutron decays into a proton and an electron ⬭

    D When a beta particle is emitted a new element is formed ⬭

    E A beta particle is a high-energy electron ⬭

Ionisation

2 Fill in the missing words to complete the following sentences.

    a) .... particles can collide with atoms or molecules that are ....

    b) Electrons are knocked out of their structure, and they form .... particles.

    These particles are called ....

3 Give two types of ionising radiation.

    a) ....

    b) ....

Background Radiation

4 Give four sources of background radiation.

    a) ....

    b) ....

    c) ....

    d) ....

5 Explain why background radiation is not harmful to our health.

....

Nuclear Fusion & Fission

Nuclear Fusion

1 Nuclear fusion is a self-sustaining reaction. What does this mean? Tick the correct option.

    A The fusion reaction is reversible and forms a continuous cycle ⬭

    B The energy produced by fusion drives further fusion reactions ⬭

    C The products of one reaction are the reactants for the next ⬭

    D The reaction always takes place within a closed system ⬭

2 Give two examples of nuclear fusion.

    a) .... **b)** ....

Nuclear Fission

3 Name the two substances most commonly used for nuclear fission.

    a) .... **b)** ....

Nuclear Fission on a Small Scale

4 The diagram illustrates nuclear fission on a small scale.

Match statements **A**, **B**, **C** and **D**, with the labels **1**–**4** on the diagram. Write the appropriate numbers in the boxes provided.

    A More neutrons ⬭

    B Uranium nucleus ⬭

    C Neutron ⬭

    D Fission occurs ⬭

Barium nucleus

Energy released

Krypton nucleus

Nuclear Fission on a Large Scale

5 Which of the following statements about uranium fission are true? Tick the **two** correct options.

    A Energy is released in the form of heat ⬭

    B Heat energy is taken in ⬭

    C Each reaction releases a huge amount of energy ⬭

    D Each reaction releases a small amount of energy ⬭

Notes

M

4:15

30

4:45

Chemistry   C   ISA 25%   4
                      A
Physics   B   4

Biology   C   4

Periodic Table

Key

| relative atomic mass |
| **atomic symbol** |
| name |
| atomic (proton) number |

Example:

| 1 |
| **H** |
| hydrogen |
| 1 |

1	2											3	4	5	6	7	0
																	4 **He** helium 2
7 **Li** lithium 3	9 **Be** beryllium 4											11 **B** boron 5	12 **C** carbon 6	14 **N** nitrogen 7	16 **O** oxygen 8	19 **F** fluorine 9	20 **Ne** neon 10
23 **Na** sodium 11	24 **Mg** magnesium 12											27 **Al** aluminium 13	28 **Si** silicon 14	31 **P** phosphorus 15	32 **S** sulfur 16	35.5 **Cl** chlorine 17	40 **Ar** argon 18
39 **K** potassium 19	40 **Ca** calcium 20	45 **Sc** scandium 21	48 **Ti** titanium 22	51 **V** vanadium 23	52 **Cr** chromium 24	55 **Mn** manganese 25	56 **Fe** iron 26	59 **Co** cobalt 27	59 **Ni** nickel 28	63.5 **Cu** copper 29	65 **Zn** zinc 30	70 **Ga** gallium 31	73 **Ge** germanium 32	75 **As** arsenic 33	79 **Se** selenium 34	80 **Br** bromine 35	84 **Kr** krypton 36
85 **Rb** rubidium 37	88 **Sr** strontium 38	89 **Y** yttrium 39	91 **Zr** zirconium 40	93 **Nb** niobium 41	96 **Mo** molybdenum 42	[98] **Tc** technetium 43	101 **Ru** ruthenium 44	103 **Rh** rhodium 45	106 **Pd** palladium 46	108 **Ag** silver 47	112 **Cd** cadmium 48	115 **In** indium 49	119 **Sn** tin 50	122 **Sb** antimony 51	128 **Te** tellurium 52	127 **I** iodine 53	131 **Xe** xenon 54
133 **Cs** caesium 55	137 **Ba** barium 56	139 **La*** lanthanum 57	178 **Hf** hafnium 72	181 **Ta** tantalum 73	184 **W** tungsten 74	186 **Re** rhenium 75	190 **Os** osmium 76	192 **Ir** iridium 77	195 **Pt** platinum 78	197 **Au** gold 79	201 **Hg** mercury 80	204 **Tl** thallium 81	207 **Pb** lead 82	209 **Bi** bismuth 83	[209] **Po** polonium 84	[210] **At** astatine 85	[222] **Rn** radon 86
[223] **Fr** francium 87	[226] **Ra** radium 88	[227] **Ac*** actinium 89	[261] **Rf** rutherfordium 104	[262] **Db** dubnium 105	[266] **Sg** seaborgium 106	[264] **Bh** bohrium 107	[277] **Hs** hassium 108	[268] **Mt** meitnerium 109	[271] **Ds** darmstadtium 110	[272] **Rg** roentgenium 111							

Elements with atomic numbers 112–116 have been reported but not fully authenticated

*The Lanthanides (atomic numbers 58–71) and the Actinides (atomic numbers 90–103) have been omitted.

Cu and **Cl** have not been rounded to the nearest whole number.